My *Weird* Dreams

By David N. Greaux

VOLUME I

Written…
Designed…
Text Editing…

by David N. Greaux

© 2022
Herstellung und Verlag:
BoD – Books on
Demand, Norderstedt
ISBN: 9783756836000

``My *Weird* Dreams``

By David Nelson Greaux

About the Author

I was born on 18 April 1959 in Saigon, South Vietnam, now Ho-Chi-Minh. Raised on Saint Thomas, U.S. Virgin Island. Joined the military in 1977 and landed in Germany where I have been living since. Got married on 6 June 1980 (D-Day, how can I forget) and our son was born on 17 December 1986.

Intro

What do Dreams Mean? Well, that depends on what you read and whom you talk to. Everyone has their interpretation of dreams." Don't let Dreams affect your life, let Life affect your dreams." I am no expert on dreams and never claimed to be.

Have you ever woken up in the mourning and thought, dam, that was a weird-ass dream? I used to do that all the time. And of course, I would have to tell my wife about my dream the next morning whether she wanted to hear about it or not. Even as a kid I could remember my dream the next day. And let me tell you, I have had some weird-ass dreams. Dealing with sex, violence, friends, drugs, death, fun times...have had them all. Short dreams, long dreams. Most of my dreams are short ones. I usually would only remember a part of my dream. Some of my dreams are dull ones. I do not always remember my dreams and I would most often have various short dreams. I always use to joke around with my wife that I need to write down some of my dreams. Well at the age of sixty-two I decided it was now or never...

CHAPTER ONE

Winter Dreams

"We were hugging and greeting each other when I thought, should I be doing this?"

A good friend and mentor "Bill" passed away. I was at his house talking to his wife showing my condolences.

All of a sudden, I was standing next to a window trying to urinate on the floor. I stopped myself thinking I cannot do this.

I think I was naked, not sure. I then went to their bathroom, but I had a problem closing the door to the bathroom. It was an extra-large door and hard to close. I finally got it close.

I lifted the lid of the toilet and was shocked that the toilet was filled with leftover food, mostly cooked noodles. But I had to go so I urinated in the toilet.

I had to flush a couple of times before I could get the toilet empty.

Shortly after that other people started showing up also to express their sorry for "Bill" passing away.

Some people I recognized, others I did not.

We were hugging and greeting each other when I thought, should I be doing this?

I don't know some of these people, what about Covid 19?

"He said he was feeling a lot better, then we gave each other a long hug, a man hug"

Wow, this was a roller-coaster ride.

Where do I start...I was involved with a racist white group that was looking for recruits, but of all races, I was confused.

We were there for a day to get information about the organization so we could decide whether to join or not.

I did not like what I saw and did not plan to join, but I had to play along because these were some shady people and feared for my life.

While at their clubhouse a vehicle showed up, and out came about four-five men.

One of them was my friend Bill…again.

So, I saw him, went up to him, and asked what he was doing there, he was supposed to be in the hospital bedridden.

He said he was feeling a lot better, then we gave each other a long hug, a man hug!

"She was wearing a sexy nightgown and a little embarrassed."

I was in bed with my wife.

She was wearing a sexy nightgown and a little embarrassed.

I asked her what was the problem. She said she had been to the doctor to write her sick for the day to be with me in bed and was feeling guilty about that.

Before I knew it, she was stroking me, then…then I woke up! Dammit!

"I was wearing these thin see-through beige jogging pants"

I was at my old workplace, or I should say a building next to my workplace.

I worked at a hospital, in logistics. It was "bring your spouse, friend" to the work day. I brought my wife.

It looked like we were staying in my old military barracks.

We were sharing a room together with other people, civilians, and military personnel.

I was getting bored and was waiting to get a call from work that they had something for me to do.

I told my wife I had to go for a walk, I was bored stiff.

So, I leave the room and go into the hallway, it was a huge hallway. At least twenty feet wide went on forever.

I started walking toward the end of the hallway.

I guess it was the janitor, he was moving giant furniture around from one room to the next, almost bumping into me a couple of times.

I finally get to the end of the hallway. I am standing in a room with a large mirror. I am looking at myself thinking, what the hell do I have on?

I was wearing these thin see-through beige jogging pants. I said I cannot have people seeing me dressed like this, I have to get back to my room.

I finally get back to my room where a former work colleague is laying on one of the beds. She had just gotten out of surgery.

Her head was totally shaved, and she was telling everyone the surgery went well, she was going to be just fine.

The next moment I am driving my car on the freeway.

Everyone is driving like crazy people.

Cars almost smashing into each other, cars driving in the wrong direction causing near misses.

I guess I survived.

"I found myself walking down a narrow dirt path"

I was attending one of my veteran organization conventions.

I was in my hotel room, which actually looked like a room from my old military barracks. About five guys to a room with bunk beds, loud and noisy.

I did not recognize anyone in the room. I had to get out of there.

I found myself walking down a narrow dirt path towards where I figured was the convention center.

It must have been in or by an airport because I could hear a woman yelling out, if you are on the flight so and so, you need to hurry because the flight is about to leave!

There was an elderly couple walking in front of me pretty slowly struggling with their luggage, I finally was able to pass them up. I was thinking, should I help them or not?

I thought not. I was in a hurry to find where everyone was.

All of a sudden, I was sitting in a stadium. It was like a ballpark stadium.

Sitting in front of me were three young guys. They were a little rowdy.

Behind me were some young girls giggling and making jokes.

I was feeling really tired, so I decided to sleep for a while.

I woke up and decided I had to find out where the convention hall was, so I started walking away.

I was checking my pockets to make sure I still had my wallet and keys. All there.

Then I realized I had left my baseball cap at my seat.

I turned around and saw that one of the three guys that were sitting in front of me had found my cap and was trying to hide it from me.

I walked up to him, grabbed it from him, and said, I think that belongs to me.

I walked away, looking back a couple of times making sure they were not following me.

I now found myself sitting in a bar having a drink by myself.

I never did find out where the convention was being held.

I then notice two people I knew, Mike and Ed sitting at a table with another guy.

I heard Ed say that he needed some trophies for the children performing at the convention and that he could perform a magic show for them.

Mike said he only lived a couple of hours away; he could drive home quick and pick up some trophies for him.

I got up and walked toward their table.

I said to them, If Ed said he can do a magic show, I know he can.

Ed and Mike got very serious really quick and were looking at me pretty weirdly.

Ed said to me, I think we were having a private conversation here. I got the message and walked away.

"My wife did not show any remorse for me passing away"

In this dream one moment I was alive and well, then without warning I passed away.

Like real life. I realized I was dead because I was walking around and doing things without anyone noticing me.

I would talk to people with no reaction. I would touch and try to grab people with no reaction.

I could feel myself getting frustrated.

Finally, I decided that was the way it is and would just have to live with it…or die with it?

I started getting comfortable with the new me. I tried messing around with people, trying to do pranks on people, to no avail.

They could not see me, feel me. I was dead!

My wife did not show any remorse for me passing away, had found someone else, and was moving along with her life.

Which I found was pretty dam quick after my passing away.

I saw her one day rearranging my old military uniform, taking off my medals, and putting on the medals of her new husband.

Apparently, he was retired military and was financially very well off.

I saw her bragging to someone about how wealthy he was and enjoying her new life.

Made me feel like crap.

"All of a sudden, the owner of the dog pulls out a sledgehammer"

It was raining and cold.

I was standing by a car, and the engine of the car was out of the vehicle resting on the floor.

My father was standing next to the motor telling me that we have to lift the motor over the fence.

I said wait, I have to put on gloves, my hands are cold, and the engine is slippery with grease and oil.

I walked to the back of the car and opened the trunk to see if I could find some gloves, but no luck.

As I walked back to the front of the car, I noticed my mother was sitting inside the car.

We then tried to lift the engine over a fence. Of course, it was too heavy, and we could not lift it.

"Then I told him, you know me, I say what I mean."

I was in a room with someone I knew years ago. Not really a friend, but someone I knew from one of my veteran's organizations.

I had written an article about him, and he was thanking me for what I said about him although we were not the best of friends.

Then I told him, you know me, I say what I mean.

I found myself walking by myself in a rough neighborhood.

I kept looking behind me, I was fearing for my life and wanted to get the hell out of there.

I could see someone walking toward me with a pit bull on a leash.

The dog was getting out of control and trying to break loose to come to eat me, I guess.

All of a sudden, the owner of the dog pulls out a sledgehammer and smashes down on the head of the dog.

Blood spattered all over the place and the dog was dead.

"The walk to the elevator was long and dangerous"

I was in a foreign land. The local situation had just turned from bad to worst.

It was not safe anymore to be there. I was with a group of people and had to get out of the country as soon as possible.

We had to walk to an elevator that would bring us up to an airport to catch a plane out of the country.

The walk to the elevator was long and dangerous.

The buildings along the road were destroyed and debris was fallen down from the buildings.

We reached our destination but had to climb a high wall and a tree to get to the elevator.

We finally got to the elevator. There were only two buttons to push, the first and tenth floor.

Two of us got into the elevator and pushed the button to go up.

We got to the tenth floor and wanted to get out when I noticed I forgot important paperwork which I needed where we got on.

I told my friend I had to go back; I could not leave without them.

One moment I was on my way down in the elevator to get my paperwork, the next moment I was being paraded down a street with the group of people I was with, transparent mesh hoods over our heads.

We seemed to be prisoners. Why, how we got there I did not know…

"At this point, we were in the state of Wyoming"

I was underway with my wife and some friends with a camping wagon to an American Legion national convention in Arizona.

At this point, we were in the state of Wyoming. No idea why Wyoming.

The locale American legion department was having their own convention and I guess we were there for that?

Anyway, to get to where the convention was being held, we had to walk through a sort of obstacle course, which was proven to be very dangerous and complicated.

I finally made it to the convention center.

Once there I was trying to get a ticket to enter the convention center, but no one was there to sell the tickets.

When I asked how I can buy a ticket they said that only the state legion commander can sell the tickets for entrance, and he was not here yet.

I was getting excited because I wanted to buy some legion articles before going to Arizona for the national convention.

A crowd was gathering and also getting anxious to get in.

Finally, the commander showed up and started selling tickets for entrance to the conference center.

As I approached him, I wanted to show him my membership card, but he did not want to see it.

He welcomed me and gave me my entrance ticket along with five pennies.

Before I could ask him why the five pennies, I woke up.

"All of a sudden, a man came running in and started swinging with what I guess was an axe killing everyone he could"

I was out shopping with my wife for some cat food.

We were in a store and my wife was mixing different cat foods in a bowl that she had opened, I do not know why.

The salesperson came over to us and said that she needs to mix the food with very hot water.

My wife was skeptical at first, but she put boiling water in the bowl and started mixing everything with her bare hands.

She screamed with pain when her hands hit the boiling water. Her hands were scorched.

The salesperson said it is your own dam fault, putting your hands into the hot water.

My wife was furious. She started screaming that she would sue the store, the salesperson told her to do so, and my wife demanded that she see the boss.

I pulled out my mobile phone and started taking pictures as evidence.

My wife grabbed my arm and said let's get out of here.

The next moment we were in the house of the pet store owner.

We were standing in the kitchen which looked just like my mom's kitchen.

I looked in one of the other rooms and a cat had thrown up all over the floor. It was a mess.

The house was packed with people just hanging around.

The owner of the house was setting up a buffet in the backyard for everyone there.

Then the door opened up to the back yard and someone announced that the buffet was now open for everyone.

We all started at the same time pushing through the doors to the buffet. It was chaos.

Finally, outside people started looking for someplace to sit.

There were a lot of tables set up with a lot of food for everyone.

I noticed there was also a bus in the yard and some people were getting on to go to another location.

I was like, where the hell are they going? Never got an answer.

"All of a sudden, a man came running in and started swinging with what I guess was an ax killing everyone he could, they were zombies."

I was now in what seemed to be a large train station.

The stairs going down to the trains were packed with people walking in some sort of a trance.

All of a sudden, a man came running in and started swinging with what I guess was an ax killing everyone he could, they were zombies.

While another man yelled out, you need to get out of here!

There are too many of them, save yourself.

The man with the ax ran out of the building saving himself.

"When she bent down towards me, I gave her a kiss on her cheek"

I was back in St. Thomas U.S.V.I., we were visiting with some friends for what seemed to be a Thanksgiving Day dinner.

It was a bit chaotic, people going in and out of the house, sometimes loud.

I walked into the kitchen; it was a huge kitchen with at least six ovens.

All I could see was meat…and more meat. There was a turkey, must have been thirty-forty pounds. Bunch of hams and at least fifteen meatloaves.

There was a lot of food for a lot of people.

I was taking a nap in the living room, might have been after eating dinner. When I heard one of my female friends calling my name.

I made believe I did not hear, she called out my name a couple of more times, but I did not respond.

She then came into the living room and came over to where I was laying down, she came over to shake my arm because she was starting to worry.

When she bent down towards me, I gave her a kiss on her cheek.

She was startled and asked why did I do that. I just said I was happy to see her after all these years.

She then laughed and went back into the kitchen.

We were all again in the living room watching the TV when another female came and knelt right in front of me to watch the screen and blocked my view.

I was like, what the hell!

I made a joke saying yea, all the women like to kneel before me.

She laughed, got up, and started to walk away.

I then noticed that she had soiled her pants and she did not even realize what had happened.

I pulled her over to the side and discretely told her she needed to get cleaned up and change her clothes.

"One day I woke up and I was working as a police officer"

I was working at a local police station, as an errand boy, getting the mail out, making coffee, and so forth.

One day I woke up and I was working as a police officer.

We were either undercover cops or detectives of some sort.

Everyone was in civilian clothes.

One thing I do know is no one liked our captain.

Our police chief was a female, and she had a thing against the male personnel.

You could tell in how she talked to them and the way she would look at them, she did not care that everyone knew how she felt.

What was weird, was that we spent most of the day listening to phone calls. I guess we were working on a case, and we would do this every day.

Was getting a little boring.

We could not leave the station for lunch and would have to work late into the evening, listening to phone calls. Everyone was getting annoyed, and something had to change.

Then one day everything changed. We got a new police chief.

"He" was a lot better to get along with. Work conditions improved and we were again one happy working family.

"Since when did I have a safe room?"

I was lying in bed late at night when I thought I had heard noises in the house.

My wife was sleeping beside me.

I started thinking to myself, what if someone is in the house?

I have no weapons to defend myself and protect my wife.

I got up and looked around to find something I could use to defend myself. I found an iron rod.

I went back to bed and laid the rod under my pillow where I could grab it quickly if needed to beat off any intruders.

It was a sleepless night. They never came.

The next morning, I got up and walked towards the kitchen to make myself some coffee, the wife was still sleeping.

I noticed a young girl walking back and forth in front of our front door.

I could see her because we had large glass doors. She seemed to be waiting for someone, keeping an eye out for someone.

Then I realized, she was waiting for the burglars to get here so they could break into the house.

I ran back to the bedroom and told my wife to get up and get dressed, we have to get into the safe room I told her.

Saferoom? Since when did I have a safe room?

Anyway, we ran into our safe room, locked the door behind us, and waited.

After waiting for a long time, we decided we had to get out soon. But we had to get out of the house in case the buglers were in the house.

Then we noticed a large window high on the wall, this was our chance to make a getaway.

We piled some furniture on top of each other, climbed up to the window, and made our escape.

"She just looked at me and was smiling and giggling"

I was again in a strange foreign land

There was a war going on. The local military personnel seemed to be all women. No men.

A battle had just finished, and the women warriors were marching their male prisoners away to be sent back to the country that they came from.

One of the prisoners was screaming, "we will be back, and then it will be a woman who dies".

I started looking for someplace to spend the night.

I found one room to stay in, but it was on the second floor, and I had to share it with other people I did not know.

There were no stairs to get up to the apartment, so I do not know how I was getting up there.

I do know that to get back down I would have to jump off the balcony onto the ground.

I found myself in a different room of the apartment laying on a couch looking at the TV.

There were other girls in there also, when one decided to come and lie beside me.

She did not say anything.

She spoke another language that I did not understand. She just looked at me and was smiling and giggling.

I went back into the living room, but there was no place to sit. The room was crowded with people.

I went to another room and asked if I could have a chair to sit on.

A woman sitting in there told me I could have a chair.

She wanted to give me a double folding chair which was not very stable.

I told her I cannot take it, I think I am a little too heavy for it.

She just started to laugh.

"I was laying on the bed and feeling aroused"

I found myself in a small town. I guess I was visiting family.

I was in the center of the town walking around.

I was about to cross the road when I noticed that the traffic was blocked at an intersection.

There was a wooden pallet, made into a chair blocking the cars from passing.

I walked over to the pallet and decided to move it off the road so that the cars could pass.

I was going to throw the pallet on the side of the road when I decided I would keep it for myself. It looked cool.

So, I started dragging the pallet back to where I was staying.

The pallet started falling apart in my hands.

I said, "what am I doing, this is a piece of junk". So, I threw it away along the roadside.

I continued to the house where my family was living.

I got to the entrance of the house, it was a large balcony.

I rang the doorbell but got no answer. I rang again and again, but still no answer.

I now had to go to the bathroom. Real bad. I could not hold it in anymore.

I looked around, but I did not see anyone, so I urinated on the floor of the balcony.

The problem was that I could not stop. It just kept on and on.

Finally, I was finished, and the door opened up.

It was supposedly my younger brother, but I did not recognize him. He let me into the house.

He brought me a bedroom and said I could spend the night here. He then left the room.

I was laying on the bed and feeling aroused.

I started masturbating.

All of a sudden it felt as if someone was watching.

I looked towards the door, and I saw someone peeking through the door.

I quickly stopped and covered myself with the blanket.

The person came in and said that everyone was leaving, and it was time to go.

No mention was made of what I was doing.

By the time I got outside the family had left on a bus.

My brother told me I could drive in my car and meet them there.

There? I did not know where they were going.

So, I jumped into my car and drove off looking for them.

CHAPTER TWO

Spring Dreams

"I thought I had found a good hiding place in a small room and was safe"

I found myself on a boat hiding and frighten.

It must have been a freight boat. I think I was in the machine room.

There seemed to be people looking for me.

I thought I had found a good hiding place in a small room and was safe.

I knelt down in the corner of the room. All of a sudden, the door of the room opened up by itself.

I could see a man on a platform talking to his crew members.

He was telling them "We have to find the stowaway".

I was thinking, please do not look in my direction. He would then see me.

At that moment he turned his head in my direction, his eyes got larger, and he yelled to his people, "there he is, get him".

The last thing I remember was running to get away.

"Turns out she worked on a military installation"

I was visiting my younger sister.

She lived in a large building complex with a multi-culture community. It was a mixture of "the hood" and "Woodstock".

I was surprised how everyone got along so well with one another.

We were walking around, and my sister was introducing me to all her neighbors. It felt like one big happy family.

She had to go to work and said I could tag along if I wanted to.

I said sure. Turns out she worked on a military installation.

She was not in the military but worked as a civilian contractor.

I never did find out exactly what her job was or what she did.

"It was strange seeing these old friends once again"

I was attending a conference of one of my veteran organizations.

There were a couple of people I did not recognize. People I had never seen before.

There were also people there that had already passed away.

It was strange seeing these old friends once again.

I know we were not in Germany.

What country we were in I do not know.

"Maybe there was someone in the house?"

I was awakened at night when I thought I heard a noise coming from the living room.

I sat up and thought I had seen a light on at the entrance of the house.

Maybe there was someone in the house?

I was about to get up to grab my revolver when I released it was the moon shining into the house. Which makes it look as if a light was on.

I snugged under the sheets and went back to sleep.

The next day I was walking toward the kitchen when I noticed the front house door was partially open.

I heard someone outside in the front yard.

I went to see who it was.

A little boy from the neighborhood was riding his bicycle up and down making a racket.

He had on a Halloween mask.

When I asked him what he was doing, he said he was waiting for my grandson to come out and play with him.

I told him that he did not live here and would not be coming to visit today.

He did not respond and just kept riding his bike up and down.

I figured he would just leave after a while and go back home to his family.

"We were sitting around in the living room, talking and reminiscing about the good times we had together."

I found myself visiting with the wife of a friend who passed away a couple of months earlier.

We were sitting around in the living room, talking and reminiscing about the good times we had together.

She pulled out a box with old pictures and we started looking at them.

She said she wanted me to have them to remember him by.

"People were running in a panic trying to get to safety"

I was working in a large factory.

There were hundreds of workers, with people walking back and forth. Very chaotic.

I do not know what we were producing, but it was very loud with huge machinery and the smell of oil was in the air.

There were security personnel who kept order and were there to make sure everyone worked safely.

One day the security personnel were nowhere to be found.

Management tried to contact them but could not reach anyone.

The workers noticed that and took advantage of the situation and just started doing whatever they wanted to do, not paying any attention to the safety rules.

All of a sudden, a fire broke out in one of the machine rooms.

The machines had been overloaded and I guess they just overheated.

The security personnel finally showed up.

People were screaming at them; they need to get the workers under control.

This will turn into a disaster.

It was too late. You heard a huge explosion and a fireball rolled through the factory.

People were running in a panic trying to get to safety, and they were all running in my direction.

I was like, do I go in and try to help those who were hurt, or do I try to save myself?

It was too late to do anything. I ran to try to save myself.

I finally got outside of the building and was looking for somewhere or something to save me from the blast when the whole building blows up.

Then I found an easy chair, it looked soft and comfortable. I said to myself, I am properly going to die from the blast anyway, I might as well be comfortable when it happens.

As I was sitting there, waiting for the big Boom! I was thinking, dam, so close to retirement and this happens.

What a bitch!

"My cat was on the warpath. A warpath against me"

My cat was on the warpath. A warpath against me.

As I would walk past my cat, he would wait, then he would make his move.

Before I knew it, he would spring on my left foot, always my left foot.

He would bite my big toe. Almost taking the whole toe into his mouth.

I would grab the back of his neck, squeeze, and pull on him until he would let go.

Most of the time it would take a while before he would let go.

I guess if I was smart, I could have worn shoes around the house. Guess I was not very smart.

This went on for a while. It was not a one-time thing.

This one time I could not get him off my toe by grabbing him as I would.

I had to take my thumb and push down on his eye until he let go of the pain.

I enjoyed the fact that my cat was the one in pain, not me.

"Did I get on a bus for this short ride?"

I found myself on a bus with some friends of mine. I did not know where we were going.

No sooner than we drove off, we were at our destination.

It was in the same town where I lived.

I was like, what the hell? Did I get on a bus for this short ride?

As we got off the bus, everyone walked over to a hotel where we were to spend the night.

I was thinking, this is silly. Why am I staying in a hotel in my own town when I live right around the corner?

"He did not realize they were just using him for his money, not because of friendship."

I was hanging out at my favorite food stand.

A friend of mine had started up this food stand selling steak sandwiches. They were the best sandwiches in town.

The idea was so simple and profitable. He was making a killing. He could hardly keep up with the demand.

Every day people would be lined up to buy their steak sandwiches.

Unfortunately, my friend had a great idea to make money, but he had no idea how to manage his money.

Instead of putting money back into the business to improve it and keep it up, he was too busy spending all the money that he was making off the food stand at the locale disco.

He would invite his friends to party with him, picking up the tab every night.

He was enjoying his popularity. He did not realize they were just using him for his money, not because of friendship.

One day I got word that my friend had to close down the food stand and leave the country.

Apparently, he got caught doing some illegal business and the deal was, that either he left the country, or he would have to go to jail, for a very long time.

So, he took the choice of leaving the country.

I thought to myself, this was my chance.

With my friend gone, I could take over the food stand.

I knew who supplied him with the steaks, I had a cook who was willing to work for me.

This was my chance for a new beginning.

"I ran up the stairs and tried to find that dumb cat."

I was in the city. I do not know why I was there.

And to make it more unclear, I had my cat with me. It was in a cat transportation box.

I was getting ready to leave the building.

I put the box down with the cat because I needed two hands to open the door to get out. It was a very heavy glass door.

I got the door open and, was standing outside.

I turned around for a split second and the door slammed shut. It was locked and I could not get it open again.

I looked in through the door and I saw my cat had gotten out of the box and was running up the stairway out of sight.

I was like, what am I going to do now?

Luckily some people were coming out of the building and opened it and let me in.

I ran up the stairs and tried to find that dumb cat. Of course, I could not find him.

I did run into some friends who were sitting at a bar having some drinks. They invited me to sit down and chat some.

It was like I forgot all about the cat.

I asked how I get a drink around here. There was no bartender.

They said I had to use the automatic drink dispenser that was at the corner of the bar.

I said you all are kidding me, right? They assured me they were not pulling my leg.

I walked over to the drink dispenser, looked at it, and thought, how the hell does this thing function?

Finally, one of my friends came over and explained how it worked. It was so simple. I felt so stupid.

We all sat back down at the bar and were bullshitting about old times.

We were there for hours. Had a great time and forgot why I was in the building in the first place.

I never did find my cat.

"That was it. I yelled at him and told him he could kiss my butt!"

I was walking down a dark road very early in the mourning.

I knew I was in a bad neighborhood.

I saw three men standing in the shadows. I did not have a good feeling about this.

They started to approach me.

I did not know if I should run or stand my ground. I decided not to run and hope for the best.

As they came up to me, they asked if I was lost and if I needed help.

Boy was I relieved!

I told them I was looking for a workshop to fix the wheels on my desk chair, which fell off.

They pointed me in the right direction.

It was still early so I had time to get there before they opened up. So, I went on my merry way.

By the time I got to the store, there were about three customers in front of me. So, I waited patiently for my turn.

It took forever.

It was finally my turn and the salesperson said he had to take a break. He would be right back.

By the time he returned there were more people to be served.

I thought it was my turn, instead, he started serving a woman that came after me that he apparently knew.

That pissed me off!

I told him what the heck is going on! I was here first.

He ignored me and continued serving the other woman.

That was it. I yelled at him and told him he could kiss my butt!

I then stormed out of the store.

So, there I was. My problem was not solved, stranded with no transportation because I walked to the store.

Boy, was I pissed!

I could not find a taxi, so I started walking home.

I was passing by a restaurant when I saw the husband of my wife's cousin having lunch with his son.

I went in and told him I was glad to see him and asked if he could give me a ride home. He said sure, no problem.

They were finished with lunch and were getting ready to leave anyway.

As I was waiting for them, I could not overlook these huge avocados in a barrel in the corner of the restaurant.

I had never seen such big avocados in my life.

I never did get the wheels for my chair.

"I found myself walking through a small seaside town."

I was making a delivery to a doctor's office.

I had boxes of medicine…and a huge beefsteak?

I was walking through the doctor's office, looking for someone to accept and sign for my delivery.

There were many patients waiting to see a doctor.

I had a hard time getting through the crowd with my packages.

I finally found someone to help me out.

I was giving her the packages and she was marking them off her roster. Then she saw the huge steak.

She said, "what the hell is this?". This is a doctor's office, not a butcher shop!

I tried to explain to her that it was also on the delivery list.

She refused to accept it and said I needed to take it with me.

I thought to myself, I guess I know what I am eating for dinner today and got the hell out of there.

"I was enjoying the peace and quiet walking along the waterfront."

I found myself walking through a small seaside town. I felt like I was somewhere in Italy.

It was not a tourist attraction. I was almost all by myself.

I was enjoying the peace and quiet walking along the waterfront.

I decided to walk towards the center of the town to check it out.

I was walking through an alley when all of a sudden, it turned into a large furniture store.

It was as empty of people as the rest of the town.

I could see one employee stacking some boxes in the corner of the store.
Then I realized I was smoking a cigarette.

I thought, oh shit! What should I do?

I decided to just keep on walking towards the exit and to get the hell out of there before someone noticed me.

"There I was. Just hanging on for my dear life."

I was spending some time with my wife at a hotel.

Do not know where it was. It did have a casino and was seemly packed.

I did notice there were many Asian and Black people staying at the hotel. And they were pretty rowdy.

There were people arguing and fighting all over the place. Physically fighting.

I was walking by the slot machines where there was an Asian man smoking a cigarette.

Apparently, there was no smoking allowed because one of the employees was telling him he had to put out his cigarette right away.

He did not like that and jumped on the employee and started fighting with him.

All of a sudden, the guy's buddies also jumped in swinging away.

Then the police showed up. It was chaotic.

I thought this is too much for me.

I had to get out of the hotel for a while. Get away from all this craziness.

I left the hotel to walk around for a while.

I forgot to tell my wife I would be gone for a while. I was sure she would not notice I had stepped out for a while.

As I got outside, it was as crazy as inside the hotel.

I could not believe it. What the hell was going on, where the hell was I.

It looked like a run-down neighborhood, with a mostly Black population.

There were large groups of people hanging around. I did not feel comfortable at all.

I decided to walk around anyway.

I was walking up this steep hill when I heard music and a large group moving down in my direction. They seemed to be wearing uniforms.

It was a school marching band.

The closer they got to me the louder the music got and there seemed to be more and more people gathering.

They were pushing me to the side to get through.

I decided to take off in one of the side alleys to get away.

It was getting too dangerous.

I was running and running when the alley just ended.

It just ended with what seemed to be a one-hundred-foot drop into the water.

I almost fell into the water.

What saved me was a rope hanging down which I was able to grab onto.

There I was. Just hanging on for my dear life.

Finally, someone came along and said to hang on, he was going for help to save me.

Next thing I knew I was back at the hotel.

My wife asked where I had been all this time.

She was looking all over for me but could not find me.

I said I was just out for a walk. Nothing much happened.

"As I looked through the window again, the cars parked on the streets were gone. Blown away!"

I was spending some time with friends from the family.

I was only planning to stay a couple of days. I was just passing through.

They lived in the city, in a large high-security complex.

I was just hanging around the house watching some TV passing the time away with their children. A boy and girl.

The parents said they had to go shopping and if I would not mind taking care of the kids while they were gone. I said no problem.

I was looking out the window watching them getting into their car.

As they opened the back of the car, I could see about five, or six computer screens in the car.

The weird thing is that they were all on.

I asked the kids what the deal was with the screens in the car. They did not have an answer for me.

All of a sudden there was a loud blast!

As I looked through the window again, the cars parked on the streets were gone. Blown away!

There were people laying on the streets and in the driveway of the building. Some seemed to be dead, and others were injured.

I comforted the children, telling them their parents were okay and that they would be home soon.

The truth being I had no idea when and if they would ever be coming home again.

Time passed by and I noticed these three young guys trying to get into the building.

They motioned to me to let them in. Apparently, they had forgotten their house keys.

I knew they lived in the building because I had seen them around before. They were military guys.

I went down to let them in. One of the guys was pushing a shopping cart.

As he came in, he told me, not in a friendly manner, while you are here you can go ahead and pay for the taxi!

They did not have any more money with them.

I said, excuse me. I do not think so.

They did not like my answer.

One of the guys then got into my face and started to push me telling me, that we military guys have to stick together.

I still refused to pay for their taxi.

Before you knew it, we were fighting it out.

It did not take long before I had the situation under control.

They apologized for being assholes and went along their way.

I went back upstairs to check on the children and to wait on their parents to get back home.

"That is when I told them they could kiss my ass!"

It felt like a déjà vu.

I was working as a pool boy again.

I was looking for a part-time job, so I went and applied at the local pool facility.

The job was more as a handyman than that of just a pool boy. I was taking care of the whole facility.

It started off okay.

I was just in charge of keeping the pool area clean and playing lifeguard. Although I was never trained as a lifeguard.

The owners did not care. They were just interested in saving money.

After a week or so I was told, I was also supposed to run the cafeteria.

How was I supposed to do that and do the lifeguard job at the same time?

And the cafeteria job sucked.

I had no training, no one to guide me, I was thrown into the cold water. And boy was I drowning.

One day trying to take a food order from a family I finally cracked.

It was a simple thing. They wanted to know the price of some chicken nuggets and I had no idea how much they cost.

They were getting as frustrating as I was.

There was no one there whom I could ask. No menu. I was losing it.

I finally told the family I would be right back. I had to go find someone who knew the prices.

I left the cafeteria and never went back.

The family might still be sitting there waiting for an answer for all I know.

I went back out to the pool area.

My boss came up to me and told me the pool patio need some work done to it.

There were holes in the ground around the pool that need to be filled so no one would trip and fall.

It was a safety hazard.

They were just worried about being sued.

That is when I decided. They were looking for a part-time worker to do a full-time job.

Same old story. They just wanted to save money.

That is when I told them they could kiss my ass!

I walked out and never returned.

"It did not take long before they started pointing at us, screaming what the hell we were doing there."

I was living in a divided community.

There was the "white hood" and the "black hood".

There was always fighting going on between the two groups.

One day some friends decided they wanted to sneak into the Black community and take over one of their houses.

There were four of us.

I thought they were crazy and did not think it was a good idea.

But like a fool, I went along with them.

We heard that this one family would be gone for a couple of days. This was our chance.

We sneaked into their neighborhood.

We knew if anyone saw us there would be trouble.

It was obvious we did not belong there.

We broke into the house. No one was there.

I was relieved about that. I had a bad feeling about the whole situation.

After two days in the house, I decided I had enough.

This made no sense at all. What were we going to prove?

We were taking a good chance of being killed if anyone found out about us being there.

I told the other guys I had enough, I was getting out of here before this went all wrong and someone got hurt or killed.

That night we jumped into our car and hoped we could make it out of there in one piece.

The problem was that there was only one way out. That was smack through the middle of the town.

That was where all the bars were and, on this night, it seemed like everyone was out getting drunk.

We drove slowly not to attract much attention. But a car full of white guys driving through their neighborhood?

It did not take long before they started pointing at us, screaming what the hell we were doing there.

They were on to us. We stepped on the gas and got the hell out of there. Luckily, we made it out in one piece.

I told my friends, that was the last time I was going to do something so stupid as that.

"His face was getting redder and redder. He started taking off his coat and yelling, if I wanted to fight, we can do it right here and now."

I was at a dinner banquet from one of my volunteer organizations.

Some people were going to be awarded certificates of appreciation for their contribution to the organization over the past year. And I happened to be one of them.

I felt honored and proud to be one of the chosen ones.

We were standing in front of the head table waiting for the president of the organization to present us with our awards.

When he got to my name he started to laugh.

He said he does not know how it happened, but in all his years as president, he never wrote the name of a member wrong on a certificate.

He handed me my certificate.

He had crossed out my name which was misspelled with a pen and just wrote my name again by hand next to it.

I was holding it, looking at it, and could not believe that he would hand out a certificate like this and think nothing of it.

I was in shock and pissed off!

I told him, in a loud voice, you got to be kidding. This is ridiculous and so unprofessional.

I just threw it back at him and told him he can keep the dam thing. I do not want it.

I turned around and just left the room.

Later that evening we bumped into each other.

He started up that I should not have acted the way I did.

That just pissed me off more.

I then started yelling at him about how he sucked at his job, and no wonder no one respects him as our president.

That in order to gain respect, he needs to show respect to others.

He did not like that.

His face was getting redder and redder.

He started taking off his coat and yelling, if I wanted to fight, we can do it right here and now.

I said you see, a perfect example of what kind of person you are. You were not worth my time.

I just walked away.

Leaving him to wallow in his little world.

"I was thinking, dam, I should have taken off right after work instead of hanging around."

I had just been notified that I got a promotion at my job. I was the new supervisor.

I was caught off guard. I did not know I was up for the job, and because I was not really interested in doing the job.

It was a Friday, and I was hanging around with some of the guys after work.

I decided to get something to eat before going home.

One of the guys asked what I was still doing hanging around. Normally I took off right after work.

I said my wife was out shopping and would not be home till late, so I was getting a bite before I left.

I was just getting ready to leave when our boss came to us and said that we needed to meet up in the shop so everyone could be informed that I would be taking over as the new supervisor and to answer any questions that the workers may have.

I was thinking, dam, I should have taken off right after work instead of hanging around.

We all went back to the shop.

There were about twenty people there. I thought I had five people in my section.

So, the boss was talking, and I was thinking to myself, I hope she hurries up. I need to get the hell out of here.

Then she says that we have to work this weekend.

That sucked.

I already made plans to do a trip this weekend. And besides, I did not even want the job as a supervisor.

So, what do I do? Do I tell her I will not be able to work this weekend, or do I just not show up?

I said screw it, I just won't show up.

Never got to find out my decision.

"I was just shaking my head and grinning thinking...dam cat!"

Some friends had just gotten a cute kitten.

They did not have any children, so it was kind of a substitute.

They treated the kitten as if it was a baby.

I hated when people do that.

It must have been Christmas time because there was a Christmas tree set up. Balls and all.

Everything was fine, we were just hanging around when all of a sudden, the cat started to freak out!

The tree must have frightened it.

He sprung onto the tree.

All the decorations were falling off. Branches were breaking.

They were trying to grab the cat off the tree, but it was scratching and snarling like it was possessed.

I was just shaking my head and grinning thinking…dam cat!

Serves them right!

CHAPTER THREE

Summer Dreams

"I opened the door and could not believe it. All my clothes were either torn or paint was splattered over them."

I was returning back to work after being at home for over a year due to illness.

I did not leave my job on a good note, so I was anxious to see how my fellow workers would react to me coming back.

I walked into the break room. There were two people sitting in there.

I said hello and expressed I was happy to be back.

The reaction from them was what I had expected. Cold and that very happy to see me.

I thought, oh well, I just have to deal with it.

I then went to my locker to put on my work clothes. I was met with a surprise.

Someone had written graffiti all over my locker and the lock was broken off the door.

I opened the door and could not believe it. All my clothes were either torn or paint was splattered over them.

I knew they were pissed off at me, but this I did not expect.

I slammed the door shut and stormed off to see my boss.

I walked into his office and told him of the situation.

He just shrugged his shoulders and said, what am I supposed to do?

I said you got to be kidding!

So, I told him I guess I could go back home. Since all my work clothes are destroyed, I have nothing to wear.

I told him when my co-workers have a different attitude and are ready to apologize, give me a call and I will think about returning again.

I never did get that call to come back to work.

"We were driving up this narrow road when I noticed on the first floor of this one building there was no front wall."

I was on vacation with my wife and son. My son must have been about thirteen years old at the time.

My son was going through those rebellious years.

My wife was telling him something when he came back with a smart-ass answer.

That just pissed me off. I automatically raised my hand to smack him in the mouth.

Lucky for him he moved to the side, and I missed hitting him. But he did behave the rest of the day because he knew he had pushed us to our limits.

A friend came to pick us up in his van to drive us around to see the town.

He was acting a little funny. I did not know if he had been drinking alcohol or not.

I was not sure if I wanted him to drive us around or not. But after a while, he was back to his normal self, and I figured it was safe for him to drive.

I was sitting in the front passenger seat watching a portable TV set waiting for us to take off.

I guess that was annoying my friend because he turns on his car radio full blast. So, I just turned off my TV.

We finally took off.

We were driving up this narrow road when I noticed on the first floor of this one building there was no front wall.

There was a martial arts class going on and you could see them training.

I noticed an elderly woman, who must have been at least eighty years old, training with a very young boy. It was amusing to watch.

She was kicking that young kid's butt.

"That is when I shoved him off with both hands, screaming at him."

I was going on a short unexpected vacation with the "guys".

Where we were going and for how long was a little unclear.

When we got to our destination it was not exactly what I expected.

It was an island in the Caribbean. The streets were dirty, and the people walking around looked as if they belonged in prison.

Getting to our "hotel" was like walking through a maze. The winding streets and one-way roads. I was happy to get our destination

Our rooms were another disappointment. We were ten, fifteen guys in one room. And it was a free for all. You took whatever bed was free. First come, first served.

I was there less than fifteen minutes before I was tested. Some guy tried to grab my arm to follow him.

I just shrugged him off and asked what the hell he wanted. He did not say anything, just stood there looking at me.

As I walked away, he tried to grab me again. That is when I shoved him off with both hands, screaming at him.

I told him he needs to get the hell out of my face or else! He did not bother me again.

I decided I needed to get out of that place for a while. I needed some fresh air. My friend and I took a walk to explore the island.

On our walk I noticed some African men talking to tourists trying to lure them into dark alleys. It was obvious they wanted to rob these people.

They were all very skinny, just skin and bones. As if they had not eaten in months.

We were thirsty so we decided to get ourselves some beers.

We were walking when these two drunks started to follow us.

They wanted one thing, our beers.

They started to get aggressive. Coming right up to us and tried to grab the beers out of our hands, like they were possessed.

I threw my beer in the bushes nearby, trying to get them away from us. It worked.

They were like zombies. The beer was pulling them in the bushes like flies on crap.

We got the hell out of there.

On the way back to our "hotel", we met up with some other guests staying at the same hotel. We started walking together.

We were having a hard time finding the hotel when those African guys showed up that we saw earlier.

They tried to get us to follow them up this dark road, saying this was the way to the hotel. I knew it was the wrong way.

I told the guys what they were up to, that we needed to get as far away from them as possible. They were trouble.

So, I told them thanks but no thanks. We would find our way back on our own.

We finally found our way back. I was happy to get to our hotel again.

Even if it was a crappy hotel.

"It was all good until I pulled out a new pair of underwear to put on."

~ 46 ~

I found myself in a room changing into some other clothes.

I was not alone.

A friend of mine was there and… U.S. President Biden.

How and why the three of us were there I did not know.

I felt a little weird. But I figured if it did not bother them why should it bother me?

We all started getting dressed.

It was all good until I pulled out a new pair of underwear to put on.

It was like four sizes too big for me. It was the only one I had so I put it on anyway.

We were all finally dressed and ready to go.

I never did find out why we were there and where we were going.

"I was able to grab him and get my wallet back. At the same time, I was yelling out "police, police"."

I was at an outdoor fest with my wife.

There were many people, music, food, and drinks. There were also some suspicious people.

It was not long before I was approached by a group of young men. I knew this would not go well.

As one of the guys was trying to start up a conversation with me, I noticed the others starting to surround me and getting too close for comfort.

All of a sudden, I felt a hand reaching for my back pocket.

Before I knew it, he pulled my wallet out of my pocket. I tried to grab his hand, but it was too late.

He tried to hide behind his buddies, but I knew he had my wallet.

I was able to grab him and get my wallet back. At the same time, I was yelling out "police, police".

Lucky for me they were close by and came to my rescue. They took the whole bunch down to the police station.

The next day I had to go to the court where they were to be tried for stealing.

As I got there, I decided to ask about an old friend who used to be on the force and worked there.

For some reason, they did not like the fact that I was asking about him and were getting a little pissed off.

I decided to let it be.

The court session started.

They must have had a good lawyer. They were all let go, not guilty.

That got me mad, and I started to get a little loud and screamed that this was not right, how could they get away when there were so many witnesses that saw them do what they did?

In the end, I was escorted out of the courthouse and almost charged with unruly conduct.

"There was blood all over the place. My lips were all cut up."

I was in the bathroom. I wanted to trim my mustache.

For one reason or the other, I decided to use a pair of large scissors this day instead of the small scissors that I would normally use.

Big mistake.

Before I knew it, I cut my lip.

I started to bleed.

But instead of stopping, I continued to try to trim my mustache.

Bigger mistake!

There was blood all over the place. My lips were all cut up.

I just stood there looking into the mirror, thinking what the hell did I just do?

Funny thing was, I was feeling no pain.

I just cleaned up the mess and went about my business.

"All of a sudden, their balcony collapsed with the weight of all those people on it."

My wife and I were living in a small apartment downtown.

There was a music fest going on in our town, and since we lived downtown, we had some friends over to have a little party ourselves, music for free.

We had a full house.

We had a lot of plants all around our apartment, and with all the people in there it was getting too crowded for me.

I could not move without bumping into a plant or one of our guests.

It was driving me crazy.

Finally, the music started, and people started moving out to our balcony to enjoy the music.

Right across from our balcony there was a small band set up and playing music.

We lived on the third floor.

Their balcony was full of people. Jumping and dancing to the music.

People were screaming.

You could hear them crying for help and crying.

Everyone in our apartment was okay.

You could hear the sirens and help was on its way.

We all just went back inside and continued with the party as if nothing happened.

"At that moment he took the pitcher in had in his hand and poured the contents over my head. It was salad dressing."

I was working in a factory. It was loud, dirty, and smelled of petroleum and diesel.

Our shift workers were assembled before work. Our boss wanted to talk to us.

She was chatting away. I was not paying attention.

I was cleaning up my area.

I was off for a couple of days, and I had some food in my locker that I needed to throw away.

There was a bag of sliced bread that was all green with mildew, and cans of fruit that were left open and had funny things growing in them.

It was disgusting.

Then our boss decided we would play a game to get everyone loosened up and in a good mood for work.

She started flinging old toast bread around the room like a frisbee.

We were supposed to catch them.

She was taking this too seriously and was getting mad when someone would not Catch them, and they dropped to the ground.

All I could think was, you must be kidding. Is this real?

Suddenly, I found myself back home in my garden.

I was walking around inspecting my plants.

I could not figure it out, but all my plants were dying.

The leaves were turning black. Drying up and dropping off the trees.

It was depressing, so I told the wife, go ahead and get dressed, we are going out to dinner.

A delicious meal always brightened up my day.

When we got to the restaurant, we met some friends and decided to get a table together.

We sat down and ordered our meals.

Our food finally came. I ordered a side dish of salad and noticed it was pretty dry. Not enough dressing.

When the waitress came around, I asked if I could get some more dressing for my salad. She said no problem, will be right back.

After a while, I saw whom I presumed was the kitchen chief walking toward our table.

He did not look very happy and was carrying a large pitcher in his hand.

He stopped at our table, and asked if I was the one complaining about not having enough dressing on my salad?

I said I was not complaining, I just liked a lot of dressing on my salad.

At that moment he took the pitcher in had in his hand and poured the contents over my head. It was salad dressing.

He yelled out "I hope you have enough dressing now!" and went back into the kitchen.

We were all in shock.

Very calmly I told my wife to take out her camera and take a picture, then to call the police so I could press charges against this maniac.

I never did find out how this ended.

"All of a sudden, a man in the crowd pulls out a handgun and shoots into the air screaming "the parrot", "the parrot"."

I found myself vacationing in Egypt.

It was pretty chaotic.

There were crowds of people on the streets. It must have been a local holiday.

They were singing and danced.

Suddenly, a man in the crowd pulls out a handgun and shoots into the air screaming "the parrot", "the parrot".

I guess he was trying to shoot a parrot that was flying by.

For whatever reason, I never found out. He missed.

Some parrot feathers did fall from the sky.

Later in the evening, I was walking along the beach.

I noticed some local people in the water.

They were wearing some weird clothes and seemed to be trying to pick up a conversation with the tourist.

They looked different than the regular locals, they were very dark-skinned, not light-skinned like the locales that were dancing in the streets earlier.

They just looked and acted differently.

I was hesitant to make contact.

Finally, I got the courage to go over to them and make small talk.

They were friendly and interested in where I came from and wanted to know more about me.

One of them had a snare drum with him and started playing on it.

When he was finished, I told him that was cool, and I was also a drummer.

"The screeching, the blood, it was not a pretty sight."

I found myself strolling through a zoo.

I was standing in front of the lion's lair thinking, something is wrong with this picture.

Inside the lion's lair was a second cage.

It was filled with smaller animals. Birds, rabbits, pigs, etc.

I figured there was a reason for this.

All of a sudden, the door of the smaller cage opens up.

The lion noticed this right away and plunged like lightning into the cage.

He was tearing at the animals in the cage. Killing them all.

The screeching, the blood, it was not a pretty sight.

Shortly after all the animals were dead and the lion was enjoying a feast.

I walked away in shock.

That evening I was at a friend's house for dinner.

We were done with eating, and I said I would help with the dishes.

I went into the kitchen. I found a small television and turned it on.

I started washing the dishes when suddenly, my hands were full of blood.

I am looking at my hands thinking what the hell…where is all this blood coming from?

I looked down at the plates from dinner, they were all covered with blood.

"I opened up a drawer on my desk when I noticed there was a bundle of money inside."

I was kind of dating this one girl. She was a good childhood friend.

Well, we were more good friends than dating.

I think I wanted it to be more than it was.

One day I was just sitting around waiting for her to visit.

When instead this one guy shows up, sits right next to me, and started up a conversation.

I knew the guy, and everyone knew he was gay.

I started getting uncomfortable and was getting ready to leave when my female friend showed up.

I was happy to see her.

I suggested we leave and go for a walk.

I just wanted to get away from this guy.

Next thing I knew I was at work.

I was working on a military installation.

I never quite figured out what my job was.

I had a desk out in the open, not inside a building.

One day there were some people doing some work on water pipes close to my desk.

It was getting late, and I was putting my stuff together to call it a day. Time to go home.

I opened up a drawer on my desk when I noticed there was a bundle of money inside.

I thought, with all these people walking around, and I could not lock up my desk, I need to take the money with me.

But the more money I took out, the more money I found.

I had no idea where all this money was coming from.

Finally, I had all the money in my bag and was ready to leave.

As I was leaving one of the workers noticed all the money in my bag and asked me what I was doing with all that money.

I just answered I was taking it to my boss for safekeeping.

"There must have been at least fifty suits hanging in my closet."

Our son was getting married.

There was a lot of commotion in our house getting everything ready before the guest arrive.

The mother and grandmother of the bride-to-be showed up and started redecorating all over the house.

They were not happy with the decorations and decided they were going to change everything.

They started exchanging curtains, rugs, tablecloths, everything.

I said I did not care. As long they were finished before the guest arrive.

I let them at it.

It was time to get dressed. We had a super large walk-in closet

My son was in there putting on his suit.

I asked him if everything was okay and ready for the big day.

He said he was ready and could not wait till it was over. He did not sound very enthusiastic about the whole situation.

I was looking for the suit I wanted to wear but could not find it.

There must have been at least fifty suits hanging in my closet.

Finally, I found the right one, got dressed, and went to wait for the guest to arrive.

"Two nurses were looking for me. Apparently, I forgot about my physical therapy appointment."

I found myself in a large building complex about six, or seven stories high somewhere on an island.

There were bars, grocery stores, medical facilities, shopping stores, and just about anything you needed.

You never had to leave the building if you did not want to.

I was down by the pool, of course, they also had a pool, taking care of a child who was in the pool.

I did not know the child and did not know why I was in charge of taking care of him.

I was also pushing around a wheelchair.

The funny thing was that the child did not need a wheelchair to get around and neither did I.

We were getting ready to leave when I met a friend, who had passed away a couple of years ago.

We started to talk about days passed as if he never left us.

He then noticed I had a menu in my hand. It was a drink menu.

He asked about it. I told him it was for a bar I was planning to open up soon in this same complex.

He thought it was a good idea and wished me luck in my new endeavor.

As we were walking along some paperwork fell out of his hand. They were medical records.

He said he was here to see some doctors about some medical problems he was having.

It was obvious he did not want to talk about it, so I changed the subject.

All at once, I heard someone yelling my name over and over.

Two nurses were looking for me. Apparently, I forgot about my physical therapy appointment.

I was thinking, dam, it must be important for two nurses to be looking for me.

I dropped everything, my friend and the child I was supposed to be taking care of and went with the nurses.

We got into an elevator and went up to the physical therapy room. *Wish I knew how that went, they were pretty hot!*

CHAPTER FOUR

Fall Dreams

"I shook her a couple of times to bring her out of her trance."

I and the wife lived in a house together with a family with two small children.

Apparently, the mother of the children was not capable of taking care of the children.

Every time the children crapped in their diapers they would start yelling out "nurse", "nurse", to come and change their diapers.

My wife was a nurse and took on a part-time job taking care of the children when needed, like when their diapers were full.

This night was no different.

They always seemed to call out when my wife finally was asleep.

I heard them calling out, so I tried to wake up my wife like I always did.

This night was different. I had a hard time waking up my wife.

She finally woke up but was in a trance.

Her eyes were wide open but would not respond to me.

She was starting to freak me out. This was not normal at all.

I shook her a couple of times to bring her out of her trance.

Finally, she came back to herself. What a relief.

The next day we told the other family they had to move out. It was getting to be too much.

They moved out and we had our lives back like it used to be.

"My wife did not hesitate and just walked into the water with the clothes she had on."

I found myself at a party sitting at a table with my wife, a school friend from my wife, and a buddy of mine.

It was strange that my buddy was there alone without his wife.

Apparently, she was on vacation by herself.

We were talking about a garden party we recently had at our house.

My buddy kept going on about this one girl that was there. That he has not seen her since then and wondered how she was doing.

I could see this was irritating my wife's school friend.

By the look on her face, I know she was thinking, why is this guy asking about this girl, he is a married man.

Shortly after my wife and I got up and said our goodbyes.

As we got outside, my wife noticed there were plants on sale.

She walked over to look at the plants.

She then grabbed this one large plant and started walking away.

I was like, hey, aren't you going to pay for the plant?

She said no, they are free, we can take what we want.

I did not argue with her. I just followed her down the road.

After walking for a while, we ended up down by a beach.

I was wondering what we doing there.

My wife did not hesitate and just walked into the water with the clothes she had on.

She had a large net on a pole and was trying to catch something in the water.

I never found out what she was trying to catch or where she got the pole from.

I decided I might as well go in the water too.

Although I had shoes on it was still hard to walk along the shore.

There were black clams all along the sea floor and on the rocks along the sea shore. Thousands of them.

The water was crystal clear, and I could see everything under the water.

After a while, we decided that we had enough water for the day and was time to go home.

"He said in three days I was to go undercover."

I was sitting in a bar with a friend having a drink.

A man came up to us, it was Will Smith, a known movie star. He said he would like to talk to me in private.

We walked outside. He asked me what time was it.

I looked at my watch and was amazed

I had a Rolex on. With different knops and gadgets. Where it came from, I had no idea.

He said that was a gift to me for my acceptance into the firm.

I applied for a job in a "Man in Black" organization months earlier and finally was accepted.

I thanked him and asked when do I start.

He said in three days I was to go undercover.

I would receive all the information I needed in the mail.

Three days came and left. I never did receive any information about my new job.

I tried to contact someone from the "firm". Could not get hold of anyone.

It was as if they never existed.

What a disappointment.

"Finally, after a while, he gave up and walked away from us screaming he would be back."

I was visiting a city with some friends.

We were walking around enjoying the scenery and minding our own business when we noticed an intoxicated man following us around.

At first, he was not a problem, but then he started to harass us.

He wanted to bum a cigarette. When no one gave him one he then started asking us for money.

After no luck with that, you could see he was getting irate and pissed off.

Finally, after a while, he gave up and walked away from us screaming he would be back.

He was cursing at us and waving his hand in a fist.

We were relieved he was gone, and we could continue to enjoy our visit.

After about an hour, our drunk showed up again.

This time he had what we thought was a large dog on a leash.

As he got close to us, we realized it was not a dog but a leopard.

What the hell was he doing with a leopard?

Now we were really starting to worry and scared as hell.

He said that he would be back and wanted revenge for us not giving him cigarettes or money.

All of a sudden, he let the leopard from the leash and the leopard jumped on one of our friends mauling him.

It was not a pretty site. The screaming and blood all over the place.

We were helpless and we could do nothing to help our friend. We ran for our lives.

We ran into a nearby store and locked the door behind us. We called for help.

It seemed like forever until help arrived.

By then it was too late for our friend.

The police shot the leopard and took the crazy drunk guy into custody.

We continued our tour of the city.

It was as if this never happen, and it was only a dream!

"They were vicious and dangerous"

I was again underway with one of my veterans' organizations.

We traveled in a group to a strange land that I had never been to.

We were supposed to meet up with other members.

We reached our destination, and the people were acting strangely.

It was like a big secret why we were there and what we were supposed to do there.

It was not like our regular get-togethers.

I tried to drum up conversations with some of the people I had just met.

You could tell everyone was on edge about being there for one reason or another.

We were at a market place I guess, and three were giant fish-like creators slithering along the streets.

They were vicious and dangerous.

They were eating each other and swallowing people whole.

Their mouths were large enough to swallow a man in one gulp.

One almost got me. I was standing next to one of these creators when another one scooped down and ate another fish that was directly next to me.

I was lucky. I ran to find shelter.

"My wife said that they frequently came by to work in the garden"

My wife and I were renting a house right next to the military warehouse where I use to work years ago.

One day I was on the balcony of the first floor when I noticed a vehicle had driven into the driveway and parked halfway on a flower bed.

I called out to my wife, I told her she needs to come out here and look at these people in our driveway.

She came out and said she knows who they are. They were the owners of the house.

I asked what the hell they were doing here.

My wife said that they often came by to work in the garden. I said, okay. They could come by every day as far as I am concerned.

Later that evening the wife asked them if they wanted to stay for dinner.

I said what are you doing? We do not have anything to offer them.

Thankfully they could not stay for dinner, they had other arrangements.

The next morning there was a delivery sent to the house.

It was about fifty bags of cement. I was pretty sure the delivery was meant for the military warehouse next door.

But the driver of the truck said no, it was the address he was supposed to deliver to.

Luckily, we had a large storage room behind our garage. Why I do not know.

So, we had them put the cement bags in there.

Later on that day we had another delivery.

This time it was two APCs, Armored personnel carriers.

I knew what the driver was going to say so I said, just park them on the road in front of the house on the road.

My son passed by the house and told me he could probably sell the APCs.

So, he organized a truck, loaded them on, and drove away with them.

Never did find out what happened to them.

I decided to walk over to the military warehouse. I wanted them to take the cement bags off my hands.

They would not take them. I was stuck with fifty bags of cement.

What are you going to do?

"Our country had fallen into a civil war"

I was walking along a beach with some friends, enjoying the sand and the cool water on our bare feet.

It might be the last day together. The next day we were to go to the battlefront.

Our country had fallen into a civil war. Between the privileged and deprived

We decided to go out to dinner. The last supper?

Where did we end up? KFC.

The next morning, we were up bright and early, packed and ready to go.

Since we did not belong to a regular military unit, we had to find our own ride to the front.

I happened to see a bus ready to move out when I noticed the commander of the troops was an old friend of mine.

I asked if we could tag along with them. He said no problem, as long as we do not interfere with their operation and his troops.

I said no problem. We were on our way.

When we reached our destination, we tried to get off the bus. We could not.

The bus was packed with soldiers and equipment.

We could not get to the door to get off.

We were getting frustrated and mad screaming "we need to get off now!"

The next thing I knew, we were back home again.

All my friends were safe and sound.

Never did find out who won the war.

"The situation got worst, and we got into a fistfight"

I was sitting in front of my computer at work.

I did not know where I was working or what my job was.

All of a sudden two men were standing in the back of me. Taunting me and basically getting on my nerves.

The situation got worst, and we got into a fistfight.

Needless to say, I got my butt whooped. Real good.

A couple of days passed.

My wounds were healing. They never caught the guys that beat me up.

One day I was passing past the boss's office when I noticed someone being interviewed for a job.

It was one of the guys who beat me up.

I slammed the door open and told my boss sorry to interrupt, but this was one of the guys that attacked me.

The guy then jumped up and ran away before we could call the police.

He was never apprehended.

Time had passed. My wounds were healed, and my life was back to normal.

I was planning a party at my house and was looking forward to it.

As I got home from work some guests were already at the house. I had to work late that day.

I was walking around the house welcoming my guest when I noticed two men that I did not know standing by my bar.

There were the two men that attacked me a couple of weeks prior.

I walked over to them and asked what the hell they were doing in my house. They had some balls, and they need to leave.

The bigger guy, whom I had found out was known as the karate kid, said that they were there because his friend did not get a job where I worked. And they did not like that.

I did not see them any more that evening and presumed that they had left the party.

The next morning, I woke up and wanted to clean up a little from the party.

I walked into the living room and there they were.

They said they were not leaving until they were ready to leave.

At this point, I worried about the safety of my family.

I went back to my bedroom and grabbed my revolver…then I woke up.

"He was wearing a dress, had a blond wig on, and yes, high heel shoes"

I found myself in a small town. I did not recognize where I was.

There seemed to be a meeting going on with one of the Veteran organizations that I belong to.

We were not holding our meeting in a building, but out on the street.

It was weird. Why were we sitting around on the street? No one seemed to know.

I recognized some of the people there. Some I had not seen in many years.

The head table with our officers was set up on the sidewalk.

They were a little hard to see because the sidewalk was elevated.

Then I heard one of our members making a remark about our adjutant.

He was saying how his high heel shoes look good on him.

I was thinking, What? What the hell is he talking about women's high heel shoes?

I finally got a glimpse of the adjutant; I could not believe my eyes.

He was wearing a dress, had a blond wig on, and yes, high heel shoes.

He was just going about his business like it was normal to be dressed like that. I was in shock.

What was more disturbing was that everyone else there seemed to think this was normal and was not strange at all.

It was getting late in the evening, and I was getting a little anxious.

I was all dressed up and was waiting for my wife to go to a local disco. Something I normally do not do.

I do not know what she was doing but it was taking forever for her to get ready.

I finally got fed up and told her I am taking off, I would see her later whenever she gets there.

Never did find my way to the disco.

"I do not need this crap and said I am getting the hell out of here."

I found myself standing on a corner of a street with my wife and a friend.

We had just seen an accident.

A huge truck was coming around the corner and did not slow down.

He ended up smashing into another car. Fortunately, no one was hurt.

For some reason, we decided that we needed to renew our insurance on our car and the insurance building happened to be right across the street.

We walked over and registered at the front office, told them why we were here, and were instructed to go into the waiting room and wait until our name was called.

It was a large waiting room. Most of the seats were taken.

My wife and friend found a free seat.

The funny thing was, as I would approach a free seat, the person sitting next to the free seat would either put their bag on the free seat or would lay down across a couple of seats to stop me from sitting next to them.

This went on for a while. Finally, I got fed up and told my wife they could kiss my ass.

I do not need this crap and said I am getting the hell out of here. I will be waiting outside when she was finished.

As I was walking out the door the receptionist mumbled something like I should not be talking to my wife like that.

I turned to her and screamed she needs to mind her own dam business and does not know what the hell she is talking about.

"Besides a pile of garbage, there was a dead cat, a squirrel, and some mice."

I was visiting with a friend of mine.

We were just hanging around when he asked if I could help him in the kitchen.

I said no problem. We went into the kitchen when I noticed it smelled a little funky.

I asked, dam man, what is that smell?

He said I know. It has been like that for a while, and we cannot figure out where that bad smell is coming from.

That is why he needs my help.

He wanted to move the refrigerator forward so that he could clean the back of it.

It was a big double-door fridge and quite heavy. He could not move it himself.

We started moving the fridge forward, and the smell was getting worse.

We could not believe what we saw behind the fridge.

No wonder it was smelling so bad in there.

Besides a pile of garbage, there was a dead cat, a squirrel, and some mice.

How the hell they got back there he did not know.

I found myself at a local hardware store.

I was getting ready to leave when I noticed my car was blocked in by a huge delivery truck.

They were unloading some pallets and there was a commotion going on.

The one warehouse worker was yelling at them "what the hell they were doing?".

They were not only blocking the cars in the parking lot but also the one driveway into the yard.

They just kept unloading their truck not listening to what the supervisor was saying.

They finally were finished and were getting into their truck to drive away, when they realized, they were supposed to drop off the pallets in the back of the warehouse.

They just laughed and said, "not our problem, the pallets are all unloaded, and we are out of here".

They just drove away laughing.

The supervisor ended up jumping on a forklift and bringing the pallets where they belong.

Shit happens.

"The woman was very attractive, wearing a black leather uniform, and dark sunglasses, and smiling at me."

I was taking a walk with my wife and another friend through our town.

We came up to a parked money transport truck.

There was a woman behind the steering wheel and a man in the passenger seat.

The woman was very attractive, wearing a black leather uniform, and dark sunglasses, and smiling at me.

I could have sworn I knew her from somewhere.

All of a sudden, the guy in the passenger seat started waving to me and smiling. As if he knew me.

He jumped out of the truck and came up to me yelling how I was doing, have not seen me in a while.

I was like, do I know you?

Turns out I did work together with both of them many years ago, in a different company.

Then he started bragging that the woman driving was now his wife.

That she was always a hot-looking woman, and now they were a couple, and he was promoted to supervisor.

I was just like, okay, congratulations. What was I supposed to say?

He offered to give us a tour of the building where they worked.

We had time to kill so we went along with him.

We were walking around when I noticed a group of guys hanging out taking a smoke break.

There was one guy, I could have sworn I knew him. Sure enough, he was an old friend of mine.

I walked over to him to say hi. We started talking about the good old days.

There was one thing that did not look right, then it hit me, he was wearing short pants. Real colorful bright Hawaiian colors.

In all the years I knew him I never saw him in shorts. He always wore jeans.

He did have a skin problem and was conscious of people looking at him because of this problem.

But it looked as if his skin problem had now cleared up.

My supervisor friend then came out of the building.

I had to look twice.

He was wearing a long sleeve shirt, but the one sleeve was shorter than the other like someone tore it off.

I wanted to say something, but I figured if he did not notice it, why to bring it up.

It was getting late. We said our goodbyes.

I promised to come back again when I was in the neighborhood so we could chat some more about the old days.

"Funny thing was, I did not panic. It was like, shit happens."

I was outside in my yard cleaning my pool.

My wife was getting ready to go shopping.

I kissed her goodbye and she said she would be back soon.

All of a sudden, the sky got black with rain clouds, it started pouring down like crazy.

Before I knew it the pool was filled to the rim and starting to overflow.

The water over spilled and went into the house. Before I could do anything there was about of foot of water in the whole house.

Funny thing was, I did not panic. It was like, shit happens.

As if I did not have enough to do, the doorbell rang.

I opened the door, water started pouring out the front door and the water level in the house started to go down.

It was an aunt and uncle of my wife.

I told them my wife was out shopping but they could come in and wait for her to get back. They just need to be careful because the floors were all wet.

As the uncle came into the house, there must have been some mud on his shoes.

With the wet floor and the muddy shoes, he was making a mess on the floor.

He thought that was funny.

Instead of being careful, he started stomping all over making more of a mess and laughing while doing this.

It was starting to piss me off and I got a little loud with him.

I was like, what the hell are you doing? Don´t you see what a mess you are doing? He just kept on laughing like a mad man.

Finally, the wife came home. Boy was she surprised how the house looked.

I told her she either had to get her uncle under control or I was going to kick his butt out of our house.

She was able to get him under control.

We cleaned up the house and got everything under control again.

"They had this huge rattling gun. Shells were flying all over the place."

There was a male terrorist running around the town like a madman.

He was armed with knives.

He had knives strapped to his belt, on his feet, and in his hands.

He was swinging his arms trying to cut someone, anyone, but luckily, he missed every time.

It was a miracle that no one had been hurt yet.

All of a sudden, a man came around the corner, and surprised him, grabbing him by his feet and started swinging him around like a rag doll.

He then slammed the terrorist on the ground as hard as he could.

...We thought it was over. Wrong!

He got back up as if nothing happened and started running after people again.

Finally, a SWAT team showed up.

They pulled into position, opened the one side door, and instantly started firing at the terrorist.

They had this huge rattling gun. Shells were flying all over the place. Hundreds of rounds were fired.

There was not much left of the terrorist when the shooting stopped.

Everyone started clapping. They were so happy the drama was over.

So, there you have it.

A look into my Dream World.

One thing I did discover is that I seem to dream a lot about cats

and my veteran organizations.

Do you have dreams?

Ever wonder why people dream what they dream?

Maybe now you realize that your dreams are not so farfetched,

and you are just as normal as everyone else...

Or are You?

"We were hugging and greeting each other when I thought, should I be doing this?"

"I found myself walking down a narrow dirt path"

"All of a sudden, the owner of the dog pulls out a sledgehammer"

"The walk to the elevator was long and dangerous"

"All of a sudden, a man came running in and started swinging with what I guess was an ax killing everyone he could"

"When she bent down towards me, I gave her a kiss on her cheek"

"I was laying on the bed and feeling aroused"

"The situation got worst, and we got into a fistfight"